Silver Bells

By Liesel Kippen

Balboa Press books may be ordered through booksellers or by contacting:

Balboa Press
A Division of Hay House
1663 Liberty Drive
Bloomington, IN 47403
www.balboapress.com.au
AU TFN: 1 800 844 925 (Toll Free inside Australia)
AU Local: 0283 107 086 (+61 2 8310 7086 from outside Australia)

ISBN: 978-1-5043-2372-7 (sc)
ISBN: 978-1-5043-2373-4 (e)

Print information available on the last page.

Balboa Press rev. date: 12/01/2020

BALBOA.PRESS
A DIVISION OF HAY HOUSE

Contents

1. Sounds at Christmas ~ By Liesel Kippen ♥

Christmas has a beautiful sound
Spreading love and cheer all around.
They come from near and far, you see
Warming hearts for you and me.

Sounds of laughter in the air
Joyous shrieks often rare.
Cute banter here and there
A touch of humour everywhere.

Pitter patter on the pane
Of windows eagerly receiving rain.
Silvery water droplets stain
And trails of wet bubbles quietly remain.

An audible crash near a wall
As glitter balls accidentally fall.
A voice quickly lets out a call
For someone to save one falling ball.

A rip and tear from a wrapped up gift
Beautifully adorned while carefully thrift.
Tugged in eagerness and quite swift
As ribbons and bows from its surface lift.

An excited yelp and a thankful cry
As this Christmas moment passes by.
Amorous feelings now run high
Endearing moments before day's end is nigh.

2. Pretty Sights ~ By Liesel Kippen ♥

The table was laden and wonderfully stocked
And gifts were all meticulously boxed.
Some were large, others small
None of that mattered at all.
There were interestingly wrapped cardboard cubes
But sadly, there were no bonbon tubes.
These were enjoyed very much
Pulling their ends and tugging at such.
Then waiting to see who won the tug
While all its contents toppled on a rug.
Fortunately, there were other sights
Glitter baubles and shiny delights.
Some were shimmering, others matt
Stealthily observed, they enticed the cat,
Who could n't wait to get her paws
On these, as she dropped down on all fours.
A quick stern look at her I gave
Prompting her to try and behave.
She lowered her eyes and let out a yawn
Feigning oblivion to the attention drawn.
My eyes then fell on a rugged grass shape
Intricately woven without any tape.
All these sights captivated me
Immersing me in the season's reverie.

3. What shall I have with my coffee or tea? ~ By Liesel Kippen ♥

What shall I have with my coffee or tea?
Something deliciously good for me.
A delectable tart with a decadent case
Oozing with strawberry jam at its base.
A sprinkling of icing to finish the treat
As a salivating mouth waits to eat.
The texture is crumbly, a buttery mix
Beautifully combined, the stomach's fix.
Topped with a thinly reddish glaze
This star tartlet causes eyebrows to raise.

Nestled adjacent on the wooden table
Sits other morsels, enticingly stable.
A chocolate clover lies there awhile
As its caramel petals alluringly beguile.
Soft and silky, wickedly rich
This piece of heaven makes the eyelids twitch.
Refined Swiss and dark Belgian
Over-indulgence, a sin, I would imagine.
Gorgeously glossy, this edible avalanche
Served with a teaspoon of cinnamon and a spiky pine branch.

4. Christmas Eve ~ By Liesel Kippen ♥

The night was beautifully quiet
Evening had settled in.
All the hustle and bustle
Had dissipated together with its din.
Not a creature moved about
Not a person was in sight.
Nothing that had breath
Was out on this brightly lit night.

Winter's gown had clothed the place
Her woolly carpet covered the ground.
Everywhere icicles hovered
Not a blade of grass could be found.
Shrubs were blanketed in silver lace
Shimmering in the light.
Benches sat solitary
On this brightly lit solemn night.

Lights danced from the branches
On the trees' outstretched arms.
Normally, such desolateness
Could cause anxiety and alarm.
Another glance at the speckled lights

Placed strategically along their chord,
Informed us of this wondrous eve
The birth of Christ, our Lord.

Houses were busily preparing
For their celebrations on Christmas Day.
A feeling of love abounded
And seeped through like a golden ray.
A beautiful peace transcended
Throughout this sleepy town,
While the scintillating and twinkling bulbs
Adorned the place like a jewelled crown.

5. Winter's White Ground ~ By Liesel Kippen ♥

An azure glow filled the air
Completely enshrouding the park.
Colourful shades of baby blue
Settled around well before dark.
Temperatures began pretty cold
As the day started at first light.
These soon mellowed down a tad
When morning became noon and then night.

A solitary tree stood tall and primeval
Giving character to the place.
The eyes' quick scan across the land
Showed flora had left without trace.
Not a vestige of shrub or a grizzled bush
Decorated this barren land.
Any small semblance of earthiness
Seemed extinct together with its sand.

Winter had crept in stealthily
Bringing with it chills and cold.
Sprinkling all its iciness
On its fortress and stronghold.
The alabaster shades that swept the ground
Slowly began to rise,
As little by little teardrops of snow
Tumbled down gently from the skies.

Quietly and forlornly
The tree looked down and frowned.
All of autumn's beauty
Was stifled under winter's white ground.
Crystal shapes began to form
As far as the eye could see.
Then lay there in their clumped up heap
Silvery and lethargically.

6. Snug as a Bug ~ By Liesel Kippen ♥

Deliciously frothy coffee
Simmered with cream in a mug
Painted with a snowflake
Red and particularly smug.
Nestled between delicacies
Of cakes and cinnamon treats
All made with a heart of love
For Christmas Day's eats.

The spiced rustic rock bun
With its dense and crumbly feel
Was beautifully freckled
With cranberries, raisins and oatmeal.
A tiny shimmer of silver
Caught the turned on light
As icing sugar speckles
Provided an entertaining sight.

Rosemary stalks and star anise
Sprawled untidily on the spikes
Of greenery and acorns
Which everybody likes.
Neatly tied cinnamon bark
Resembled cigars from afar
While the dimly lit bauble
Shone like a relocated star.

Silhouetted lights in the background
Lit up the cosy space
Filling it with radiance
And adorning it with grace.
This beautiful homestyle setting
With its twinkling starry lights
Such snug-as-a-bug backdrops
Are special sights on Christmas nights.

7. Quietly she sits ~ By Liesel Kippen ♥

Quietly she sits on the knobby branch
Scanning the happenings below.
Scattered thoughts plague her mind
But none of these does she show.

Kids are running on an open field
Having oodles of fun,
Playing a game of tag or chase
Out in the naked sun.

The blaring horn from a ramshackle car
Entices the tilt of her head.
An acute turn is her initial response
Then an obtuse one instead.

The clamorous horn moans and groans
Its unique growls are felt.
Excessive roars from its engine valve
Signal a loose serpentine belt.

The little bird continues to stare
At another movement nearby.
A mother cuddles and cradles her babe
Who suddenly begins to cry.

The bird's forehead etches a frown
A curious one at best.
The babe had dropped his cuddly toy
Which had toppled off his chest.

A Lamborghini whizzes past
In ostentatiously fiery pursuit,
Screeching its tyres momentarily
Like a robber who'd plundered loot.

The winged one's eyes look fixedly on
Enamoured and intrigued by it all,
Deciding whether to take wing
Or let life's moments continue to enthrall.

8. Matters of the Heart ~ By Liesel Kippen ♥

Orange breasted bird
Resting way up high
On a spindle-shaped branch
Outstretched towards the sky.
What are you thinking of?
What crosses your mind?
Has someone caught your fancy?
Perhaps a bird of a special kind?

Does she sing a lively tune
Or a sweet lullaby?
An amorous note or two
Or is she somewhat shy?
Does she hover quietly about
In your constant sight,
Or does she hide away
Like a thief in the night?

Where are your thoughts?
What plagues your mind?
Is the heart at play?
What emotions are outlined?
Could love be the traitor
That has you in a trance,
Triggering emotions
From that very first glance?

Will you groom your feathers
And preserve your elegant looks,
Or will you fly through windows
For sesame seeds in nooks?
Will you share these with her
And remove them from their shells?
If so, then might I be hearing
The sound of wedding bells?

Will there be a courtship
A lengthy one at that
As you succumb to her charms
And those eyelids that coquettishly bat?
Will you chirp and sing
For all the world to hear
Or will you huddle up closely
And serenade her quite near?

What are your thoughts?
Oh pray, do tell
For I would like most certainly
These curiosities to quell.
Indulge me this once
In your matters of the heart,
As I listen passionately
To Cupid's arrow's dart.

9. Glide through your stride ~ By Liesel Kippen ♥

Life is a constant rush
With so many things to do.
From spring cleaning the house
To cooking some meaty stew.
Dusting wooden chairs
Mopping tiled floors
Vacuuming woolly carpets
Shining knobs on doors.

The mundane tasks in life
Can be a truckload of fun
But after constant repetition
You get the pressing urge to run.
Far away from its shackles
And its padlock binding force
To the meadows out yonder
And gallop away on a horse.

The trick to its survival
Is to slowly slow dance
Not a lively fox trot
But a gliding prance.

Where you leisurely waltz
Around its restricting room
Instead of feeling suffocated
In its entrapping claustrophobic tomb.

Step forward with your left foot
Then sideways with your right.
Bring these two feet together
Then another step back with your right.
Life's moves are n't tortuous
When you know the steps to take.
Don't complicate the dance moves
Simply glide with each move you make.

Listen to the music
Wait for its accompanying beat.
Anticipate the rhythm
Rise gracefully from your seat.
Take to the dance floor
Glide imperturbably through your stride
And when you've performed your masterpiece
Take a bow and radiate with pride.

10. The Forest's Face ~ By Liesel Kippen ♥

The roots of trees hold them firmly in place
Keeping them steadfast from the winds they face.
While some have a darkness that is most severe
Others are breathtaking, with colours quite dear.
Their assorted shades sprawl across the land
Auburns, greens and coral sand.
Tints of yellow, burgundy and red
Fall's splashes are lavishly shared.
Large crimson leaves boldly display
Their intimate bond with the branches on which they lay.
They huddle up closely in a cosy embrace
While the sun's glow permeates the forest's face.

11. A Cube of Buttery Laughter ~ By Liesel Kippen ♥

A cube of buttery laughter
A cup of floury smiles.
A dash of vanilla jubilance
In the mixing bowl it piles.
A drop of entertainment
A splash of sugary joy.
Gently mix these together
To create the real McCoy.

No superficial ingredients
No substitutes for taste.
No additives or enhancements
Thrown in with hesitant haste.
No drastically diluted liquids
No randomly reduced amounts.
Nothing but the absolute best
Is what ultimately counts.

A sturdy pan of forgiveness
A generous pot of love.
An abundance of thankfulness
To God up above.

Then sift through these ingredients
And reach the perfect state.
One that is void
Of malice or hate.

When the creamy batter is ready
And has reached a silky phase.
Glaze it with compassion
And emit noteworthy praise.
Bake it the oven
And carefully watch it rise.
Then share it in fellowship
Under beautiful Christmas skies.

12. Night time ~ By Liesel Kippen ♥

Night time holds such fascination
Often more than we know.
It is filled with ambient beauty
As far as the land's views go.
Some nights are breezy and relatively dark
Others a sombre glow.
All its glittering and natural displays
At dusk, lies proudly on show.

The light from the stars gently falls
While all is quiet and still
On grassy plains and evergreen blades
Of shrubs precariously at will.
No other phenomenon can quite compare
Or create such a dazzling thrill.
Even on darkest, tempestuous nights
Nothing, its shoes can fill.

Night time secures the power
To intrigue and entertain.
All its darkened shadows
Provide an enigma, quite insane.
Its obscure and foreboding temperance
A paradox of ominous reign
For, with its all-consuming, sinister appearance
Lies a perpetually mystical and sensuously romantic domain.

13. Splashes of pink ~ By Liesel Kippen ♥

Beautiful shades of fascinating pink
Dominate the view.
Light pink flowers
Hot pink tips.
Deep pink centres
Cherry pink lips.
They all come alive on cue.

Gorgeous cherry blossoms
Spread their wings in spring.
Champagne pink stigma
Piggy pink stamen.
Baby pink pistil
Persian pink haven.
Nature's delicate bling.

Tiny little blossom buds
Lean their petals towards the light.
Spanish pink blade
Orchard pink claw.
Lavender pink splashes
Fairy tale pink tinges raw.
These tincture treasures mask themselves at night.

14. God is in control ~ By Liesel Kippen ♥

God is in control
Strange as that may seem
When a world all around
Becomes one nightmarish dream.
Hades has broken loose
With hooded eyelids we scheme.
Mankind, seemingly
Has forgotten the constituents of 'team'.

Love, care and kindness
Life's three potent forces
Have been torn to shreds
By perilous times and obscure sources.
Feelings of compassion
Humanity's innate call,
Now replaced with evil
And sights that profoundly appall.

Where is God?
We quietly ponder.
Why allow chaos
To spread way out yonder?
Why let evil prevail
And rule the roost?
Let tenderness and affection
Be given a boost.

14. God is in control ~ By Liesel Kippen ♥

God quietly looks on
At mankind's fate
And tries to fathom
Their abhorrent hate.
He patiently waits
For a change of heart
And for humans to play
Their ordained Christian part.

God waits in the wings
Sovereign in the sky,
Reigning supreme
All majestically, on high.
Omniscient, immanent
His glory immutable.
Omnipotent, omnipresent
Impenetrable and impassible.

God reigns over all
His presence dominates.
With a single motion
Life, He can eradicate.
He gives us free will
And a chance to make things right,
And to prance with puissance
From darkness to light.

This privileged opportunity
Won't always be there.
For in time, we'll realize
This offer quite rare.
If nothing is done
To show each other we care.
Then sadly and dishearteningly
Our beloved earth will lay barren and bare.

15. Scents of the Season ~ By Liesel Kippen ♥

Strong and earthy odours
Waft enticingly across the room.
Perfumed, woody scents
Float about caressingly,
Leaving gentle, musty and herby trails
That intoxicate.
From the rugged contours
Of these hardy cinnamon barks,
Clean, refreshing
And highly fragrant scents emerge.
They overpower
And cause a sudden lightheadedness.
Dark chocolate brown shades
Cover their rough, tough exterior,
While contrasting notably
With smooth, golden beige interior layers;
Delicate in appearance
But equally matched in dominant fragrance.
A flimsy sun-scorched ribbon
Clings tightly around the barks' cigar fingers.
While succeeding to capture their protruding frames
The stringy cloth is powerless to stop
Their unleashed penetrating aromas.

Woody petals protrude from dark miniature trees
Jutting outwards in sinewy oval discs
From the trees' core.
Their austere features invite sensory touch
Of their slightly jagged and gnawed edges.
A masterpiece in their design
The petals of the pinecones fold and sprawl outwards
And extend upwards.
They leave no trail of fragrance behind
But a quizzical and casual pondering
At their strangely attractive rendering.

Lying precariously on top of the wooden slab
Are scattered oval-shaped balls.
Carefully carved designs trace their hardened shells
With deep trenches running along their length.
Although adorning a solid, tenacious form
These coffee-coloured nutmeg nuggets
When inhaled deeply
Exude beautifully bold and vibrant, inebriating smells
Which are fleeting, but lingering.
Their distinctively pungent and aromatic fragrance
Add to the perfumed array that emanates.

Nestled comfortably between the rustic contours
Are silvery iced marzipan stars
On beds of ginger morsels.
From these, a mixture of fragrances permeates the air.
Nutmeg, cinnamon, maple syrup and treacle
Are all intertwined and subtly blended
To produce spicy ambrosial scents and a fruity haven
All beautifully laid out for the season's festivities.

16. Wintry Winter Wonderland ~ By Liesel Kippen

Wintry Winter Wonderland
The jolliest time of the year.
Crazy buzzing is in the air
And shedding of a joyful tear.
Oodles and oodles of excitement
Happy scenes everywhere.
Everyone is carefree
There's not an ounce of sadness anywhere.

A crispy cool breeze lingers about
Catching exposed fingers and toes.
Then nestles intimately
On an unsuspecting nose.
'Atishoo' is the initial response
As winter's dust magically falls
On icicles and surfaces
That are n't snugly layered in shawls.

This dazzling setting is a mystical delight
Which lights up beautifully at night.
Splashes of colour permeate
And intriguing shadows they mysteriously create.
Subtle flashes from the tree's lights
Radiantly sparkle and glitter bright.
Round and round the electric current flows
In circular twirls and oval rows.

Shiny baubles light up the ice
Glassy, transparent, their mission to entice.
Pastel green, blue and yellow
Creating an ambience, invitingly warm and mellow.
Plump snowmen gather around each day
To watch the dancing lights on display.
Colourfully attired in their Christmas gear
And adorned with hats that prompt boisterous cheer.

You are Angels, you are treasured
Precious, priceless, whose worth cannot be measured.
You are cherished and valued too
For all that you give and all that you do.
Your smiles and sentiments give me hope
Providing my life with endless scope.
Your warmth and compassion ignite my soul
Reviving, replenishing and making it whole.
Your hearts cascade with endless love
For which I always thank God above.
You mean the absolute world to me
I hope you are able to see.
I'm so truly blessed, amongst all of life's many things
To have you, my valued family and friends ...
Beautiful angels without wings.♥

Printed in the United States
By Bookmasters